Running Water, Living Water

Running Water, Living Water

Angela Sudermann

Copyright © 2009 by Angela Sudermann

All rights reserved. No part of this book may be reproduced or transmitted in any form or by any means, electronic or mechanical, including photocopying, recording, or by any information storage and retrieval system, without permission in writing from the publisher.

Published by WriteLife, LLC
7914 W. Dodge Rd.
Suite 384
Omaha, NE 68114
www.writelife.com

Printed in the United States of America

Photo Credits:
front cover photograph, Michael R. Mann
back cover photographs, Ed Kimmey (author portrait)
and Georges Kyrillos ("Blue Water Candle")

ISBN 978 1 60808 012 0

First Edition

This book is dedicated to
Bob, Lauren and Jordan
who have loved, supported,
and humored me through all
my adventures. I love you!

This book would not have been possible without the participation and inspiration of so many.

First, to God be all the Glory!

Now to him who is able to do immeasurably more than all we ask or imagine, according to his power that is at work within us, to him be glory in the church and in Christ Jesus throughout all generations, for ever and ever! Amen. (Ephesians 3:20-21)

Now, in no particular order…

Reid Trulson, and all of my colleagues at International Ministries. It is a joy to serve with you.

Jonathan Hilsher, who supported me as a colleague and a friend. He also pushed me, encouraged me, and was many times the conduit for God to speak to me.

Bernice "Mama" Rogers, who not only is an amazing friend, but also was an incredible support and emergency contact for the entire team…24/7 on a holiday weekend and beyond.

Mike Mann, who inspires so many to join the work of ITDP. He and his wife, Becky, pour their lives out for God and the hill tribe people.

My parents, Richard and Norma Koelling, who believe in me. My dad spent hours and hours editing this writing, molding it into something readable. Even more, he encouraged me to write down my experiences, coached me through the process, and even liked it! It's because of him that this little story is in print, for he saw some value in having the story told. My mom, for teaching me how to be prepared in all situations and being a role model for a mom and a wife. I love you both!

Thank you to David Martin, Fine Lines and Cindy Grady, WriteLife, for taking this little story further towards the reality of publication.

For anyone who encouraged me to write something down…well, enjoy! I hope this doesn't raise expectations, because I still don't consider myself a writer, just a storyteller with an adventure to share.

The team: Dale Abood, Hugh Bates, Bob Betz, Ron Devenport, Tom Gillming, John Heavin, Angela Jones, Sam Miller, Shane Morgan, Dave Peery, Waylon Woods, the ITDP staff, and the village of Huey Ngu (Baan Pa Gluay). It was a joy to serve with you and see you grow together as a team. This isn't my story, it is ours, just through my eyes.

Contents

In the beginning...   11

Part I: History, Recruitment, Preparation   13

Part II: Bangkok and Beyond   20

Part III: Bangkok   75

Reflections   95

In the beginning...

On Feb. 6, 1812, Adoniram and Ann Judson were commissioned as missionaries by the Congregational Church and set sail for India. While out on the waters, Judson began to read the Bible anew about the issue of water baptism. Arriving at the conclusion that believers should be baptized by immersion, the Judsons were baptized by British Baptist missionaries when they reached Calcutta, India, that September.

Their life-changing decision not only celebrated individual new life through baptism, but the birth of a new gathering of people, partners, churches, and a new society of Christians who would support, send and celebrate the work of mission. That movement, formed in 1814, is known today as the American Baptist International Ministries.

International Ministries has grown and evolved over nearly two centuries of ministry. The movement is the oldest Baptist mission agency in North America. Adoniram Judson was known to have said, "Our future is as bright as the promises of God." The story of International Ministries is seeing the impossible become God's promises realized. It's not just a story of God's promises to people, but also about God's power to bring people together in partnership with God and with one another.

The story that follows is about just that: Promise of a brighter future for a village; partnership between missionaries, agencies, villages, and volunteers; and possibilities of new life through the simple gift of clean running water and the living water of Jesus Christ.

It is the story of many people seen through one set of eyes. Each of us has a story to tell, and this is mine. Undoubtedly others may have seen events differently, and many things are left untold. Memories make me smile, even now, with a fondness and longing for a tiny village in northern Thailand and a few days spent there.

Part I: History, Recruitment, Preparation

"Angela, would you lead the Discovery Team to Thailand?" my boss asked, June 2007.

I can't say no, although I want to, very much. I've told him I'll train people to lead teams, I just never want to do it myself. I agree because my boss asks, I love Thailand, and I have a passion for the hill tribe people we will be serving. I will be working with Mike Mann, Global Consultant for International Ministries, American Baptist Churches, USA and his team from Integrated Tribal Development Program (ITDP), based in Chiang Mai, Thailand. Together, with our yet unformed team, we will work with hill tribe villagers to construct a water system from the source to the village that will bring clean, running water into the village. We'll also help build at least three latrines and run pipe to five stations for running water. Eventually every two or three homes will have a latrine, and more running water stations will be added.

Discovery teams are preplanned, short-term mission teams which are traditionally an intergenerational group of people from all over the United States. ITDP implements and oversees water, agricultural and sanitation projects in the most remote areas in Northern Thailand. Mike is the director, while the organization is run by highly trained hill tribe staff.

We were going to serve in a village called Huey Ngu (Baan Pa Gluay), a Red Lahu Village. The Lahu (pronounced La`-who) are one of the many hill tribe people of Northern Thailand. Hill tribe people migrated into Thailand mainly from China and Burma. They have been in Thailand for more than 100 years, but are not considered "Thai". They reside in the northern mountains of Thailand and are subsistence farmers. They do not speak Thai unless they have gone to school, which is rare for the elders of the village. When some of the younger people make it out of the village for schooling, they are able to learn Thai, earn citizenship, and either go on to higher education or make a living outside of the village. Some come back to the village to live, as was the case of the 31-year-old pastor in Huey Ngu.

    Huey Ngu, a village of 24 families, is not predominantly Christian. Eight families have become followers of Christ. The headman is not one of them, but he believes in openness to religion, and that believing in something is good. It is unusual for a non-Christian headman to invite Christians into the village to work, but this man's heart is open, and in his wisdom he knows how much running water and sanitation will improve the life of his villagers. The headman, who we called "Chief", is not Lahu, but Chinese, has been in the village forty-five years, and was in the village prior to the Lahu people moving in.

    Although reluctant to lead a team, I was able to meet with Mike in the fall of 2007 to talk about what this trip would look like. His enthusiasm was contagious, and I became quite excited about the prospect of working with him and his staff. I would be in good hands with an organization that is experienced at working with teams and is highly organized once in the village.

    As a team leader and also staff member of International Ministries, my responsibilities overlapped, which worked in my favor. I am responsible for promoting and recruiting for all Discovery Teams through the Internet, brochures, speaking engagements, and personal contacts. A pastor from southern Indiana had called our office, interested in getting his church more involved in missions. I sent him information and a video about

Thailand, and soon we had two members of the team. While I was conducting a workshop at a missions conference in northern Indiana, an attendee listed what he did prior to retirement, and jokingly challenged me to find a place for him as a volunteer. I responded by telling him that I had a place on the team to Thailand just for him. Little did I know that he, his pastor, and one of his friends were soon to be members of the team.

Mike was busy speaking in churches across the USA, touching the hearts of many. We received a call from Waylon Woods in Kearney, Nebraska. Mike had just spoken at his church, the First Baptist Church in Kearney, and he wanted to know more about the trip. We spoke, and I knew immediately that Waylon would join the team, but we needed at least ten people in total. Where would they come from? Only God knew the answer to that question, and I was sure that he was not done picking the team. A call from Oregon added another person to the team. Hugh saw an announcement for this trip on a promo screen at a World Mission Conference in Medford, Oregon, and thought, "I could do that." We added Hugh to the team in late summer of 2007, making the team a definite 'maybe' of seven members. Waylon had been busy recruiting, though, and by early fall, four more were added from Kearney, making the team total of twelve, including me.

From coast to coast and in between we came: Waylon, Dale, Sam, Tom, and Angela J. from Nebraska; Dave Ron, and Bob from northern Indiana; Shane and John from southern Indiana; Hugh from Oregon, and me. I had met two of them, and talked to two others on the phone. Of the twelve, two had been on mission trips before, another had been out of the country, but only I had been to Thailand. Why were these people called together: Because they have a heart for mission, a passion for people, and a desire to help. They understood that around the world children die every minute from preventable illnesses, many times contracted by the infected water they drink. Women spend up to four hours a day hauling heavy containers of water from a stream several kilometers away from their villages. Crops die for lack of available water except in the rainy season. Clean, running water will improve health, living conditions, and agriculture in the village. Not only were we going to help bring water to a village, but we were also going to be the face of Christ to the villagers. We would not "evangelize" in the traditional way, but we would be there, and show them that westerners from halfway around the world care about them.

As always, these trips are not all about what we can bring to the experience, but also what we can learn about another culture and about ourselves. We will live with families in the village, two to a home. All I can tell the team about conditions is to expect an extremely rural lifestyle: We will sleep on the floor; eat what the staff brings, catches, or kills; showers will be cold and either from a bucket or in the river until the water is running to the village. There will be no electricity, very little privacy, language barriers, shy people, and hard work. We won't have cement mixers, power tools, or welding torches. Everything will be done by hand with very primitive tools. Our laundry will be done by villagers, most likely in the river. We will share our sleeping space with the family plus assorted bugs, rodents, and pets. Most of all, expect to leave a chunk of your heart in the village, because you will fall in love with the people, especially the children.

During the months prior to the trip, I prepared the team as best I could from Pennsylvania. With a team age range of 30 to 77 years, there were some communication challenges. The secretary at First Baptist, Kearney, Nebraska, was my lifeline to that group, and a couple of family members kept others up to date via their e-mails. I was able to combine a trip to Kearney with a conference in Iowa, cramming as much cultural training as I could into two hours at each place. Most importantly, I was able to meet the five in Kearney who were going on the trip - a luxury for a Discovery Team leader! Two weeks later I was able to meet three from Indiana at a training workshop in Illinois. I admired their faith in me after I missed most of the main day of training because of a migraine! With a month to go before the trip, I had met half the team and was very pleased with what I saw...committed men and one woman who were preparing for work and relationship building in Thailand. The team also had a committed group behind them in the USA. Their families, friends, and congregations had been supporting them financially and in prayer and would continue to do so. An emergency contact person in place would relay news to all the families and I had colleagues at International Ministries who could help if needed. We were going to be in a village, away from satellites and cell towers, and besides...what could go wrong? Our perceived worries were not what was going to happen in the village, but whether we could get out of Chicago on our scheduled return date, the day before Thanksgiving.

  While Waylon and the Nebraska team met every week and worked out of a training manual that International Ministries had provided, the others in Indiana were also meeting and working out of the manual on their own. I was leading them through some key points via e-mail, and we were all trying to come together as a team. Everyone was packing from the list they had been sent and adding items as they were inspired. Basic necessities, host gifts, vacation Bible school supplies, warm clothing for the children, snacks, Gatorade, oatmeal and spaghetti sauce were all packed with care. Although we had some idea of what each other was bringing, none of us could have imagined the blessings that we would see once we arrived at the village.

A good friend and pastor in Ohio brought the team's story to his mission board. Within a week, a large donation was sent to Thailand for the village. By the time we arrived, two beautiful warm quilts had been purchased for each family by the ITDP staff. These were greatly needed by the families because it gets quite cold at nights during the winter months. Understand that "quite cold" is relative! When it was 60°F in the mornings, the team was wearing light sweatshirts and pants, while the villagers were bundled in the warmest clothes they could find, including knit caps. When the temperature dips to 40°F at nights, they are really cold! Our own luggage included enough sweatpants and shirts, knit caps and socks for each child in the village to have an entire outfit, and each adult to have a knit cap.

Prayer plays an enormous part in these trips. Each member has specific requests, and we have some as a team. Safety, continued good health, and strength are common requests as are concerns for the families left in the USA. My prayers included being culturally aware and appropriate; patient with the team and myself; eating whatever was offered to me; being able to physically keep up with the rest of the team; and making it through immigration and customs in Chicago in time to catch my flight to Philadelphia on November 26th, the day before Thanksgiving. That prayer would come back to haunt me!

The November 13th departure day weather forecast for Philadelphia was rain. Not a great start for me to catch up with the team in Chicago because the Philadelphia airport is infamous for delays. As I sat at the gate waiting to board, the most beautiful sunrise --oranges, pinks, purples -- glowed around the scattered clouds as if God was assuring me that all was well, and it was.

Part II: Bangkok and Beyond

Most of the team met in Chicago. Two flew from Indianapolis, three took a bus from rural Indiana, and five drove from Kearney to Omaha and flew to Chicago from there. Our Oregonian would meet us in Tokyo. After a brief stop in Tokyo, where very polite, white-gloved security officers checked us through, we boarded our flight to Bangkok. Seven more hours of flying! Ugh. After twelve hours in the air from Chicago, we were tired of being crammed into airplane seats, but still excited to continue our journey. Waylon and some others feasted at a sushi restaurant at the airport and we left Tokyo with an anticipation of what lay ahead.

We landed in Bangkok. Our luggage had been checked through to Chiang Mai, so we had our carry-on luggage and eight hours to amuse ourselves in the Bangkok airport. Ron, Hugh, John and I found the Doi Tung coffee shop. It was wonderful coffee, fun company, and our first pictures were sent back to the states. Other members of the team were scouting out the massive airport, taking pictures, sampling the cuisine from Burger King to local dishes, and grabbing naps where they could. By 5:30 a.m. we were checking in at Thai Air and getting ready to board our flight to Chiang Mai and meet Mike Mann.

We were processed through immigration and customs in Chiang Mai with little problem. Almost all of us were using a blue duffle bag, each one stuffed with a wide assortment of clothing, gifts, and supplies for the villagers. After the customs agents opened the third or fourth one, the rest of us were waved through. Mike was a welcome sight at the other side of customs with his warm smile. The team was introduced to Mike and his staff and to an airport security agent who is a believer and is familiar with Mike and his teams. We loaded our gear into the pickups, hopped in the back of the trucks, and headed off to the Downtown Inn. We would spend one night in Chiang Mai before leaving for the village in the morning. Team orientation, lunch, sightseeing, repacking and staying awake until bedtime were on tap for the day. We would rise early in the morning to head to the village, so we needed to take anything we didn't need for the village and leave it in Chiang Mai. We had too many of some supplies, so with Mike's help we sorted and packed some for the village and some for a school. After so many months of waiting, weeks of preparation, and hours of traveling, we fell asleep anticipating the day ahead.

Finally, it was off to the village! The day dawned bright, clear, and promised to be hot in the city. We headed three hours north to where it was cooler, higher altitude, and far away from life as we know it. ITDP staff and Americans were spread out in four trucks -- two trucks full of supplies and two trucks full of people.

We soon learned how amazing each member of the ITDP staff was. Talented, funny, organized, and completely dedicated to the work they were called to do. Weerasek (Rambo), Witoon (No Fish), Noppadon, Jke, Amorntep, Apichej, and Mike were all part of the team going to the village. Sompoon, another young man with the group, served as the cook. We grew to love each of these men like brothers as we worked, ate, and played together.

Travel on a Thai highway is an eye-opening experience. How many family members, including the dog, can fit on a motorcycle? What was that brightly colored, three level house on the pickup that just passed us? It was beautiful, ornate, and a casket. Aside from riding, not driving, in the left side of the car, and driving on the left side of the road, on roads that are marked for two lanes but really where six are used for driving or passing, the ride was fairly uneventful. After stopping at a sacred Buddhist cave for sightseeing, we pulled into a village to eat and to shop for rubber boots and machetes. All of this travel was on paved roads, but it would get bumpy after lunch. Really bumpy.

We soon came to an intersection where we would turn left and leave the pavement for dirt. After stretching our legs for a minute, we piled back in the trucks, and braced ourselves for the ride. This road was one vehicle wide and was extremely bumpy. Wide ditches ran parallel to the length of the road, in different locations, but never on the side. They had been made by tires during the rainy season and had since dried and hardened. Some were as much as a foot deep. Between the ditches and the rocks in the road, the curves and the up and down hill maneuvering, our skilled drivers were able to navigate the best route possible. It was still bumpy, and I worried about the folks who were riding in the back of the pickups, hoping they were not falling out! We crossed narrow log bridges, streams of varying widths, and saw God's creation in a new light.

We drove in the nest of hills surrounding us, bamboo shooting up on the roadside, poinsettias over six feet tall, and an occasional water buffalo grazing nearby. The friendliness of the people was evident when we discovered one vehicle was missing. On these mountain roads, taking a curve often entails a three point turn, and it is important to know where each driver in the convoy is. We waited and waited, but the truck behind us still did not appear. Shortly, a man and child on a motorbike passed us going down the mountain. Our driver flagged him down, spoke to him and off he drove. He had been asked to go further down the mountain and check on the truck we were missing, and come back

Running Water, Living Water

to tell us what was wrong. It didn't matter that we didn't know him, that he didn't know us, or that he may have had something pressing to do. There were people that needed help, and he was willing. This was one of our first lessons in hill tribe culture.

We were joined shortly by our last truck, and we continued on to the village. We could tell we were getting closer by the robin's egg blue PVC pipe that we could see occasionally on the hillside. Suddenly we were descending a small hill and driving into the river! What a ride!! The river was flowing well, and it was deep in some spots, but all the trucks were able to cross the river and climb the hill on the other side. Cresting the hill we could see the homes of the village and kids who heard us coming and ran to meet us.

One of the things I enjoyed most throughout this trip was seeing Thailand through the eyes of eleven people who had never been there. The food, the cities, the people all seemed to delight the team. Arriving in the village was also a treat to see through their eyes. I have served in one village and have visited many more and had some idea what to expect. We came into the main part of the village through a herd of cattle and water buffalo that were running loose in the village. Kids and dogs ran towards us. Chickens and their chicks, pigs and piglets, scattered away from us. Women peeked shyly from their doorways, and men greeted the ITDP staff with handshakes, smiles, and verbal greetings. The children quickly surrounded the trucks as we began to unfold. As we left the trucks, the kids hopped in to play, curious about all that we brought with us.

As we drove into the village we saw a few homes on our left, close to the river. Up the hill, there were a couple more, with some on the right as well. Upon reaching the crest of the hill we could see a path that led up another hill. To our left just past the path was a large fenced area which contained a house, a fenced-in garden, and a bamboo-walled latrine. Next to the house was a sturdy permanent bamboo and log table with a bamboo roof. Across from the house sat a much longer bamboo table, over which was a roof of blue and white tarp.

This common area was our "base" for the next eight days where we ate, planned, met, rested, held vacation Bible school, sang, and made and developed deep friendships. Our dirty laundry was piled there each morning. Late night adventures were shared over coffee before light broke through, and the day's adventures told and retold at night as we swatted or avoided bugs depending on how large they were. This compound seemed to be the heart of the village, a gathering place for women, men, and children, and also served as the pastor's home which he shared with his wife, two children, and – while we were there – the entire ITDP staff.

Rice was brought from the fields to a building across the common area from the pastor's house and lugged up the steps. Laundry was hung out to dry on lines strung from building to building. Dishes were washed on the second-floor porch of the pastor's house. The ever present dogs were fed from a hollowed-out log a few feet from our dining table. We had children with us at all times, almost from the moment of our arrival. What a joy!! They loved being hugged and cuddled and were constantly curious about what we were doing. The digital cameras were a favorite, and it wasn't long before they had our cameras and were taking the pictures.

Up the hill from the pastor's house was the church, a little cement block building with beautiful simple wooden pews, a brass gong to call people to church, and an opening where we could look out onto the village below. Outside of the pastor's house/ community area, turning left, were several more homes scattered up the hill. On the right were three homes, and straight ahead...a beautiful sight...a bamboo structure with blue and white tarp for sides, roof, and walls. It had three door openings, each facing a different direction, each with a stick across the opening to keep animals out, and to indicate that the space was occupied. The structure? A beautiful -- to our eyes anyway -- latrine. Three sections, each with privacy, a hole dug in the ground, and a bamboo apparatus that looked like parallel bars, perhaps eighteen inches high, placed directly over the hole. Toilet paper was hung off a wire, sometimes out of the rain. It was lovely, and a wonderful "toilet" where we could sit, not squat. It was a great gift from the staff of ITDP, built ahead of time in anticipation of our arrival. They know how well westerners handle squatty pottys.

A large structure surrounded by barbed wire sat between the pastor's house and the villagers' homes. It had huge solar panels over it, and to our western eyes looked like either mailboxes at the post office or a crematorium. It was neither. Instead, it was a "gift" from the government to supply the village with a solar-powered recharging station. Families that had a car battery (no car, of course) could take it to the recharging station to charge their batteries and get enough power to run a radio or a fluorescent light for a few hours.

We arrived late in the afternoon, dusty, tired, thirsty and just as apprehensive of our new surroundings as our new hosts were of receiving us. We were called into the pastor's yard to receive an orientation to the village. A hand-drawn map of the village was hanging from a post, complete with the locations of each host family's home, and the proposed locations of latrines, faucets, water tank, and filter tank. Each home was numbered, and a member of each host family was at the meeting in order to take their guests home. After being introduced to our hosts, we grabbed our gear and headed off to our homes. As there were only two women on the team, we were natural roommates the entire trip.

    Our hosts, Ja Ah, the husband, and Nah Play, the wife, had a typical Lahu home, built off the ground, with adequate space beneath the living area for livestock and storage. The walls were woven bamboo, the floors bamboo slats. Cooking and sleeping areas were separated by an open porch. A variety of shoes lay at the base of the ladder that led to the porch; shoes are never worn in the house. A little gate which hung halfway up the ladder was closed at night to keep invading animals out, and perhaps sleepwalking children in. Our home was nestled in a corner of the village, in the middle of the hill, close to the blue and white latrine, and had its own little haawng naam -- squatty potty. It was enclosed by a bamboo fence and was a popular hangout for the water buffalo. Three dogs lived at our house. All were fairly skeptical of visitors, and one would growl at us every time he saw us on the property.

    We set up our mosquito net, laid our packs and sleeping bags inside, and grabbed our towels and toiletries for our bath in the river. Angela and I waited for the guys to finish so we could have the river to ourselves. Bathing for the first time Lahu style was at best clumsy. To bathe Lahu style, women wear a sarong-type garment, really just a tube that can be used as a dress, skirt, or bathing cover-up. Modesty is extremely important, so women bathe with this sarong on, washing underneath it while it stays on the body. I made mine from some spare fabric I had at home -- bright yellow and white. Not a great choice to be inconspicuous!

Several attempts were made during the week to figure out just how to shower in the sarong correctly, never to any great success. In the river that night, barefoot on rocks, with the river flowing around my legs and my sarong threatening to fall off at any time, I shampooed and washed up quickly, managing to soak myself and sarong thoroughly. Had I brought dry clothes to the river, that would not have been a problem, but I didn't, so off we trekked back to the house, uphill, past the guys and the villagers, soaking wet in a clingy bright yellow sarong. The water on my feet mixed with the ever present dirt and made mud in my Crocs squish between my toes as I walked. Picking our way through the village, around children, pigs, chickens, cows, dogs and piles of manure we finally arrived at the house. Angela and I had packed vastly different things, which turned out to be such a blessing. She brought a bulk-sized pack of baby wipes, perfect for cleaning dirty feet. I brought a travel-sized container of trash bags, perfect for all the used baby wipes! Finally bathed, in clean clothes, we set out for the community area and the evening events.

After our first village dinner -- consisting of pork, rice, vegetables, and fruit -- there were introductions all around. The ITDP staff and our team were introduced to the villagers, and the water committee from the village was introduced to us. This committee is responsible for the water system. They collect 5 or 10 Baht (roughly 15 to 30 cents) from each family and save it to have money for repairs when needed. They are trained by the ITDP staff on maintenance and record keeping. Like every family in the village, they are responsible to help each day installing the water system, so they will have a good working knowledge of how the whole system is put together and operates. Anytime there was speaking between the villagers and the team, Mike or Witoon had to translate. Mike's parents were missionaries in Thailand, and Mike grew up there, learning both Thai and Lahu languages. Witoon is Lahu, and is learning English. He is 28 and is a bright, energetic, and hysterically funny young man. His passion is helping hill tribe people live off the land and use their resources in the best way possible. His English is quite good, but when he is stumped, he giggles and pushes his hair out of his eyes. We loved him right away.

All the villagers, especially the children, were curious about the mounds of brightly colored quilts stacked on the eating table. The anticipation was about to end. Each family was called up to receive two quilts. Many times the children came forward to carry the quilts back to their families and they were much less shy than their parents! We were the first westerners in the village as a group, and we looked, talked, and acted differently than anyone they had ever seen. We had brought so much stuff! Even though one of our checked bags stayed on the pastor's porch, our other bag went to the house with us. We had packed as lightly as possible, yet it still felt as though we had brought more than they would ever own. When in my life would four sets of underwear feel excessive? Yet, it did.

After a meeting with Mike and the staff to talk about the next day's schedule, it was finally time to head home, our host's home, where we could collapse until the next morning. Angela J. and I (Angela S.) had been given a room to ourselves, which we believed to be the parents' room. The parents had moved into the room next to us with their four-year-old boy.

We unrolled our sleeping bags and mats, made sure we had a bottle of water, and made one last latrine trip. It is really dark in the village at night, so we turned off our flashlights before we went

Running Water, Living Water

back into the house and just looked up at the stars. There were so many stars: big, small, and twinkling in patterns and randomly to our delight. They were close enough to touch, but not. We stood there for a while admiring God's handiwork, then headed back inside. Clumsy now, we kicked off our shoes, told the growling dog it was okay, and headed back inside.

Angela J's flashlight skimmed the room and revealed a spider whose body was about the size of a fat almond. Its legs were about three inches long, and the eyes were glowing in the beam of light. To me it was beautiful. To Angela J. it was one roommate too many and she wanted it dead, our first roommate stand-off. Angela J. wanted a dead spider. Angela S. doesn't kill bugs. What were the girls to do? Find men.

Being right off the path to the latrine, it wasn't hard to find men when you have ten male teammates and it is time to get ready for bed. Two of the Indiana guys were wandering back to their house, and we grabbed them. They, too, thought the spider was beautiful and tried to chase it out of the house to appease both of us. However, the spider refused to leave, and eventually I gave in to the other option so that my roomie could get some sleep. Scanning the room once more, we climbed under the netting and into our sleeping bags and settled in for the night.

At 4 a.m., I needed to visit the latrine again. Too lazy to walk all the way to the blue and white tarps, I opted for the haawng naam that was right next to the house. I unlocked the door, unlatched the gate, crept down the ladder, shushed the growling dog, slipped into my Crocs, and walked around the corner and into the huffing face of a water buffalo. I was awake now!! Stopping dead in my tracks, just inches from his face in front of me, and the haawng naam door to the right, I spoke softly, hoping that he understood the tone of my voice since I was pretty sure English was not his second language. I slowly slid into the bamboo structure and latched the door. I could hear him breathing outside the walls and once he brushed up against the side. I quickly finished and slowly opened the door, grateful that he was not blocking it. Thanking him for sparing me, I repeated the steps to get back into the house, remembering to use the other latrine from now on.

Pre-trip preparation of the team included a section on food. Different levels of training yielded different experiences, from trying a variety of strange foods during a training session to going to a Thai restaurant in their home towns. Whatever the experience, the important point was to taste whatever was put before you without negative comments, facial expressions, or sounds. Eating is not just about nourishing the body, but about the hosts offering part of their lives to their guests. Any rejection of such an offering is hurtful, but accepting the offering with gratitude and joy can open hearts and build relationships in a meaningful way.

The team was stretched each day to try foods whose tastes, textures, and appearance were unfamiliar, but each person was wonderful at trying new things and opening themselves to new experiences. We were provided with purified drinking water around the clock and a variety of Lahu and Thai dishes that were not too spicy. A chili paste was always available to enliven the dishes. Each meal was an adventure, but also a time to share the events of the day, get to know each other better, and rest tired muscles. For me, it was also a time to check in with the team regarding health issues, how they were holding up emotionally and spiritually, and to prepare for vacation Bible school which was held in the afternoon.

Running Water, Living Water

Our daily schedule consisted of construction, meals, vacation Bible school, and rest. We would break into different groups each day according to strengths and abilities. For the first three days, the five Nebraska team members plus one or two others would dig trenches and bury pipe. This was hard work, compounded by the location of the water source and the pipe. High on a mountaintop, the source was difficult to get to. Even more treacherous was laying the pipe into the side of the mountain. Standing level was not possible, so they were digging and balancing themselves at the same time. Waylon lost his glasses the first day, gone forever in the thick brush of the jungle. They had incentive on the first day…get the pipe to the shower so we could have running water to bathe in! They did it, and more. The "Nebraska Five" and assorted other team members would work so hard digging trenches and burying pipe that they finished a day early. While they were digging, the rest of the team members were laying and tying rebar for the base of the water tank and the filter tank.

The water system is a thing of beauty. It has no mechanical moving parts. It is totally gravity fed. To achieve this, the source must be five meters higher than the filter tank, which must be higher than the water tank, which must be higher than the village faucets. The pipe is run from the source to the filter tank where the water is filtered through rocks, charcoal, pebbles, and sand until it is clean. Once clean, the water flows to the water tank where it is held until used in the village below. It's cold but clean, and runs well through the faucets.

Remember the previously mentioned path up a hill? Those of us who chose to bend and tie rebar, because we thought it would be easier than digging, were told to pick up the lengths of rebar and take them to the tank.

"Where is the tank?" we asked, already dreading the answer.

"UP" we were told.

Forgetting my water bottle, I donned my leather gloves and with Dave and Hugh we grabbed a few pieces of rebar and started up the hill. Now, we didn't EACH have some rebar. It took all three of us to carry just a few lengths. I was in front, Hugh was in the middle, and Dave followed at the end. Up the hill we began. For two retired guys and a woman who does one sit-up a day for exercise, this was no easy task. We stopped several times to catch our breath and let our legs stop burning. Our Lahu counterparts, even the children, put us to shame with how agile and fit they were, but they never ridiculed us, and always kept us busy and useful. We worked at our own capability and with encouragement were able to improve and strengthen each day. After that morning, my big goal for the week was to get to the top of the hill without stopping. I was glad that I chose rebar that day and for the days that followed. I finally made it to the top of the hill without stopping on the third day.

Tying rebar is a bit of a dance. There is a particular pattern and rhythm to it, and once you have it, it's a beautiful thing. Staff and/or villagers had precut the wire we would need. Hundreds of rebar joints had to be tied together with these wires, and then twisted to secure the joint. Villagers, staff, and Americans were all on their knees, tying and twisting, laughing and chatting, smiling and trying to communicate. Hands of different colors, hands calloused from manual labor and hands covered with leather gloves worked side by side in the dust. Time passed quickly, and the result was a sturdy base for a water tank that would take shape in three days. We moved to the water filter to repeat the process. Soon we heard the sound we had longed for all morning…. Weerasek saying "break now, eat lunch". Mixing cement would come after lunch.

    Many times during the week the whole team would work together mixing cement and pouring concrete. This would be done early in the morning and in the late afternoon as we poured the different layers of the water tank, five in all, and the filter tank. Each time we built a layer more rebar would be added to support the concrete, forms would be built and set, spaced correctly with bamboo spacers, and then the mixing would begin. First, the bucket brigades would begin, passing rocks, then sand, adding cement, then water and sealer to properly mix the concrete in the mixing hole. Mixing was done by several people standing around the edges of the hole and pushing the aggregate back and forth with bamboo-handled hoes until it is mixed enough to stand in its middle and mix. Rubber boots were a must for this job! Once the cement was mixed, it was time to pour. Before that, however, a mixture of sand, cement, and water would be poured around the sides of the form, similar to greasing a pan.

    The bucket brigade then moved to the forms, where filled buckets were passed to people stationed at the form to pour the cement into the openings. Empty buckets were passed back through another line of waiting hands, eager to keep the flow of cement moving. As cement was being poured into the form, buckets passed back and forth and, people using long sticks tamped the cement down inside the forms, packing the aggregate and removing the air bubbles. The steady rhythm of the tamping, buckets clanging, and trowels scraping became the "music of the morning." "More?" someone would ask, until we would hear "no more!" and the assembly line movement would cease. The line would move towards the running water, and the bucket brigade would start washing the buckets for the next round of mixing.

    Moving down the hill was only slightly easier than going up. It was very steep, and when it was dry, rocks and pebbles made it slippery. When wet, the road was slick, slimy, and uneven, making a walk down the hill a challenge to find the safest path. The kids would run down the hill no matter what the conditions. I think they liked to startle us when we heard them coming up behind us! The first morning that the hill was wet, we all made it up to the top safely. I was one of the last to come down the hill when I heard a commotion in front of me, shouts of concern, then laughter. I came around the corner, still high on the hill, to see Big Dave standing up, covered with mud on his back and backside. He was walking and there was more laughter, so I did not hurry or I might be on my backside as well. About halfway down the hill I saw a wide skid mark that continued until the hill flattened out some. He slid a LONG way! At breakfast I questioned the folks who were with him, only to find that Dave's backside was his cleanest part. He had fallen face first into the mud and "slid like he was on the banana slide at a water park" down the hill. Trying to avoid Waylon, he had aimed for a tree trunk on the side of the hill. He missed the stump and Waylon, but took bunches of mud in and on his face, shirt, and pants. We were very thankful both that he was okay and that he gave us something to tease him about for the rest of the day.

    Dave was a great sport and a fun guy to have on the team. He and his friend Bob are both big men, husky and well over six feet tall. Bob is a character, too, and the two of them gave the Lahu a lot to work with when it came to teasing. Dave was nicknamed

Running Water, Living Water

"Sumo" by the ITDP staff. Other nicknames were to come as the week wore on.

While construction continued on the water system, a handful of us began work on the three latrines. These buildings have bamboo or wood posts for the basic structure. A roof is made of palm branches woven into lengths of bamboo braid. Each length of bamboo and palm leaves is the width of the structure, and there are enough of them to overlap from the lowest end to the highest. The bamboo braid is tied to bamboo beams across the top of the basic structure, securing the roofing layers to the structure. Very few nails are used, and bamboo is plentiful, free, and strong. Again, I was tying rebar, except this time with narrow bamboo strips, and the joints were over my head. My height came in handy when we were reaching the higher portion of the roof, and at almost six-feet I stand a good foot taller than many of the Lahu!

Once we had a roof to provide shade, we began the foundation. Mixing concrete and putting it into buckets was not a huge team production now. There were three Americans and three Lahu working on the bathroom. Using narrow cinderblock and concrete, we fashioned the foundation by laying concrete on the ground, squishing the cinderblock into it, and then laying the next one down and filling in the gap. Masonry at its finest! With a couple large trowels, some small trowels, a spoon and a stick, our system worked quite well. While two of us worked on the foundation, others built the throne -- the foundation for the squatty potty to sit on. Also made with concrete and cinderblocks, this square supports the porcelain bowl that is shallower than a western toilet, has places for feet on each side, and has no tank. To flush, one simply pours water down the hole where the waste goes and it all washes into a very large, deep pit. Paper of any kind cannot be put into the potty as it will not decompose like human waste. Once the squatty was installed in the foundation, a mixture of cement and sifted sand was prepared to finish the top and sides for a smooth finish.

Flattened bamboo panels, cut to size with a machete or axe and then nailed to the bamboo structure, became the walls. Finally, a door was added and voila`, the private bathroom was finished.

By default Vacation Bible School ended up being my thing. No one, including me, had volunteered to take charge of it before we left for Thailand, so I took care of it. I knew that there were supplies in the blue bags, and my mom had taught me how to be resourceful with what I had. We had pipe cleaners, crayons, four coloring books, pencils, bubbles, markers, Frisbees, balls, jump ropes, glue, foam shapes, socks, pompoms, yarn, needles and some specific supplies for cross necklaces. I also knew that it would be at least an hour where I didn't have to dig trenches or climb that blasted hill, so I was grateful for the break. Waylon offered to play guitar for the kids and we decided to teach them "This Little Light of Mine." We would teach one verse every day so they could sing it for their parents Saturday night when our team did our cultural show for the villagers. So what do you get when you combine 12 kids speaking Lahu, a guitar player who makes everything sound like a country western song, a translator with a wonderful sense of humor, and a woman who hasn't worked with kids in 10 years? Controlled CHAOS!

Mike had told us that singing, a craft, and a game would be fine. We should expect them to be illiterate, but they weren't. We could expect up to 35 for Bible school, and we had some that came every day, but mostly there was revolving door attendance.

Finally, he said that they would be amused by anything and he was absolutely correct about that! While the kids were gathering, we got out a Frisbee, which the kids had never seen, and taught them how to toss it around. They were naturals!

Waylon was amazing with the children as he played guitar and we tried to teach them the song. We muddled through somehow, getting lots of puzzled stares from the children. Witoon translated, and his presence helped the kids feel at ease. We did a second song for them, which is quite silly and involves a lot of body movement. Needless to say, the kids did more watching me waving my arms and legs, bobbing my head, and turning around than participating, but anything to break the ice! We were certainly more entertaining than anything they had seen in a while!

Our first day we told the story of God creating the animals, fish, birds, and people emphasizing God's making them special and loving them just the way they are. Pages of the coloring books, that day and every day, were hand traced with markers, so that the four original coloring books could be kept for the church's Sunday School program. After coloring and drawing, we broke out the bubbles and pipe cleaners, which make great bubble blowers. Overturned Frisbees make great bubble solution holders when fifteen kids want to use their pipe cleaners at the same time. We also had some fly swatters for mass bubbles.

Each afternoon of Bible school progressed about the same. We had a new activity -- ball or jump rope -- each day, then did music, a story, crafts, and would end with a prayer. Waylon was able to teach them three verses of "This Little Light of Mine", and they especially loved the hand motions to "hiding it under a bushel – NO," because drama and shouting were involved. One day we had a bunch of new kids attending, including the daughter of our host family. We had not seen them before because they usually attended school two-hours walk from the village, leaving the village Sunday afternoon and returning Friday, but they heard there were foreigners in the village, so they skipped school and came home two days early. This day, while most of the children were holding up their index fingers for their "little light", one little boy held up his third finger. We were sure it was completely innocent, but it was all Waylon and I could do to keep straight faces and continue singing and playing the song.

    One afternoon we made sock puppets, sewing pompom eyes on, yarn for hair, and pompom noses and tongues if the kids wanted. The older girls were quick to learn how to stitch the eyes and hair on and were soon helping the younger children. By the end of the day, each child had at least two puppets. We re-enacted the story of Zaccheus, which gave the children another crack at laughing at my antics, and they proudly wore their sock puppets home. The next morning when the kids filtered into the yard to greet us, the little guy from our house was riding a tricycle, and a splash of color caught my eye. I looked down, and saw that he was wearing a sock puppet on each foot, yarn hair blowing in the breeze, eyes bobbling with every push of the pedal. We laughed and laughed. When your toes are cold, what are you supposed to put on your feet? I wasn't the only one that was resourceful with our supplies!

    Cultural games were a fun part of each day if weather permitted. Team games were played pitting staff, Americans, and villagers against each other. The first event was Dakraw, similar to volleyball but the ball is wicker and you can only hit the ball with your feet or head. What amazing flexibility and dexterity the Lahu have, and what good sports the Americans were who volunteered to play. A great deal of fun was had by everyone watching or participating. Volleyball was the next night, where the Americans fared a bit better, and the last group sports night was relay races of carrying buckets of water on poles, and other work-made-fun events.

    Cultural learning did not take just the form of games, but dealt with everyday life. The Lahu live off the land. Men head off with their muzzle loading muskets to seek game, or go to the river to fish. One evening Witoon took some of the men to the river for some night fishing. I wasn't a part of the fishing, but we heard the commotion when they came back and the exclamation "Gone all that time and THAT is all you caught? It's a little bitty thing!" In the morning we found out that Witoon, normally an accomplished fisherman, was not having any luck snagging fish in the net the night before, and whenever he would pull in the net he would look with disgust and frustration and say, "NO FISH," and throw the net back into the river. They did come back with a fish about 2-inches long, but Witoon was dubbed "No Fish" for the rest of the week.

    A group of us experienced daytime Lahu fishing later in the week. Having no fishing poles, we were equipped with a large plastic tarp, our cement buckets, a couple of hoes, and a beautiful fishing creel. We hiked down a trail across streams, through pastures and rice paddies. Through the rice paddies I had a little helper, a young boy who took my hand every time we had to step up and then down, making sure I was okay. He was so thoughtful!! We finally came to the part of the river where we needed a ramp to get to the water. The kids found loose straw, piled it up and went swinging from the trees into the pile. The adults began walking the plank to the river. I took one step onto the plank being used for the ramp and immediately lost my balance. One foot on the plank and one foot plunging far below, I caught myself with the heel of my right hand. A couple of the guys helped me up, gave me a walking stick, and sent me on my way. I paused to pull a load of prickles out of my hand, but other than that the only thing injured was my pride. We walked upstream for a while until we found the perfect place.

Although I still don't know what makes a "perfect place," it seemed to work. The kids knew exactly what to do and began to spread out. One took a hoe and dug a ditch that would divert the water to the side of the river. Others, plus several of the men, began moving large rocks and boulders to dam up the river. Once there was a structure there, they brought the blue tarp over and placed it on the upstream side of the rock dam. Adding sticks and straw completed the dam. A second dam was constructed using more rocks. Children on the side of the river without the water diversion were digging dirt and putting it into the buckets. We formed a bucket brigade to fill holes in the second dam with the dirt and mud. This is a long and somewhat frustrating process as one hole will get plugged and a new one will sprout. Eventually, the second dam was constructed and we were standing downstream with very little water at our feet.

"OK, now fish." we were told.

We watched the kids turn over rocks and slip their hands in and out of the water. Crabs, fish, and even a small snake turned up to the delight of everyone. When the snake was found, it was immediately stoned to death by the kids and thrown into the field. At first I thought they were being unnecessarily mean, but soon realized they were protecting themselves and us. Water snakes in that part of the country are poisonous, no matter what size, and the kids know this from a very early age. The snake discovery

Running Water, Living Water

quenched my enthusiasm for poking my hands under rocks looking for fish, and I amused myself for the rest of the time by taking pictures and video. One child found a sucker fish, or algae eater, that they played with by attaching it to their faces and letting it develop suction. Bored with that, they let it go into the water again and looked for more crabs. Between what we found where the water was low and what the guys netted in the overflow stream, we had a nice little catch -- no fish was longer than about three inches, but lots of crabs and enough food to sample in the evening meal.

While we were fishing, there was also a group hunting. They caught no birds or mammals, but one of our team members caught something that would haunt him for the next four days. Eating unidentified spicy things can wreak havoc on your tummy. We were able to sample the rewards of hunting the same night we ate our fish. Earlier that morning, while we were eating breakfast, one of the men came to the breakfast table with his fresh kill, a flying squirrel. It was a beautiful animal, and he was very proud of it. The team took photos, and to be nice, the hunter plopped it on the table where our food is placed buffet style so that we could get a better look at it. At that point, I was done eating breakfast. We were told that the squirrel that evening would be part of the dinner offerings, which would be village potluck. Mike was very good that night about telling us what was hot (spicy) and what was not, and where the squirrel and the fish and crab dishes were. I tried the squirrel and found that there really isn't a deboning process. You might even say that the meat comes with its own toothpicks. As with most Thai or Lahu dishes, it tastes like the spices it is cooked in, but getting around the bones was challenging. I was told the fish and crab soup was really tasty. I love Thai food, and there were many foods that I loved that trip, and some that were good to try only once. A nice thing about potluck is that you can take a little of everything and try it without offending anyone, unless of course the dish is so hot it makes you cry, but rice is good for cooling the heat and there was always plenty of it.

      Sharing our respective cultures happened naturally all during the day and into the evenings, but on the last two days of our time in the village the sharing was quite intentional. After work on Friday, we were treated to several demonstrations of Lahu life. Prior to the first planned demonstration, we were treated to an impromptu demonstration of catching a chicken dinner. The pastor and several children were gathered around an area near our dining table, looking into some dense brush and weeds. In the pastor's hand was a handmade slingshot, and the kids were squealing, pointing, and running back and forth around the brush. Brightly colored chickens and their chicks were running out from under the weeds, and the pastor was aiming at whatever the kids were pointing at. We thought they were trying to kill a rat, but after the pastor took his first shot, it was clear that they were not after a rat but a scrawny little black chicken. The unfortunate target fled up the hill with a herd of laughing kids and a slingshot wielding pastor after it. The chicken darted back and forth, under brush, and up and down the hill. We did not see it again, but could follow its progress by where the group of children bobbed and weaved.

      To show us how villagers converted rice to food, we were taken to an area outside of a house where a wooden rice pounder was located. There were at least two of these in the village, shared by the surrounding homes. The rice pounder looks like a giant seesaw with the fulcrum closer to one side of the lever than the other. On the end nearest the fulcrum was a flat step. On the end

Running Water, Living Water

furthest away was a short, fat log attached perpendicular to the lever. To pound the rice, one would step down on the step on the short end to lift the log on the long end, and then let the step up so that the log would fall and pound the rice. This process took time and was quite strenuous. Once the husks were separated, the rice was sifted. To process the rice into flour, it was pounded once again to the desired fineness.

After leaving the rice processing, we were taken to a home to see a traditional kitchen. All in one room were the dining, family, and cooking areas. The cooking fire was on the floor in one corner, taking up about one quarter of the room. A variety of pots and bamboo utensils hung from the bamboo walls or were placed neatly on bamboo shelves. Corn was hung over the fire to be dried by the heat and smoke. One of my favorite foods was cooking near the fire -- sticky rice in bamboo, a food I was introduced to in February of 2008 and had been dreaming about ever since. Delicious sticky rice, cooked in a variety of ways in a specific type of bamboo. I had snacked on white sticky rice cooked with egg, sugar, and black beans. In the village the rice was black, straight-out-of-the-fire hot, and so tasty. No matter how it is cooked, you eat it the same way. Peel the bamboo away from the rice and a thin membrane holds the rice together - the perfect snack.

Next we left to watch different methods of trapping game and then went on to relay games. It had been a particularly hard day at vacation Bible school without Waylon and our translator and having to teach two crafts which required more hands than we had. I was exhausted, dirty, sweaty, and was really looking forward to my daily shower. Surrounded by blue and white tarp, standing on bamboo mats, my clean and dirty clothes hanging on bamboo racks, wearing my bright yellow sarong, the cold running water reminded me once again why we were there. The cold water felt good not only physically, but spiritually as well. Long after we left, that water would be there for the villagers, clean and clear for them to cook the rice they were pounding, the food they were cooking over their fires, and to clean the chickens they were chasing with slingshots. On the way back to my house from the shower, the end of the chicken's story was evident. Black feathers scattered around a large rock stained in fresh blood told it all. There would be chicken in the pot tonight.

After supper the villagers treated us to a cultural show. Most of the girls and women were decked out in their finest Lahu outfits, handmade and beautiful. Their songs, sung and accented with hand motions, told of Lahu life and how God has blessed them. From children's songs to Lahu Christmas carols, we were delighted by their beautiful voices and delicate hand motions. The children's antics amused us too. Little boys and girls are the same around the world, alternately sweet then making crazy faces and picking at each other.

We were invited to join in some of the dances, with fairly simple dance steps but beyond my mastery. For one dance, in which musicians and dancers alike move in a circle, Waylon was given a drum, and villagers used gongs and cymbals. Bean, a favorite villager among the team, and Waylon began a steady beat with the drum and gong. With a familiar twinkle in his eye, Waylon started to beat the drum faster, challenging Bean to a musical duel. The dancers' feet moved faster and faster as the audience cheered them on. Waylon and Bean were locked in a crazy competition as the tempo increased. Finally, Bean ended the dance with a final gong and the participants and audience erupted in laughter and applause.

Running Water, Living Water

When the dancing was finished, we were treated to a re-enactment of a traditional Lahu wedding. A table was set with candles, fibers, and a cup of whiskey. The beeswax candles symbolized the union of the two people, as bees swarm together. The fibers were for the spirits, and I'm afraid I don't know what the whiskey was for -- perhaps toasting. Strings are tied around each other's wrists, similar to our exchanging wedding rings. When a young man wishes to marry, he speaks to the shaman of the village and the shaman asks the bride's family for permission. Once granted, a price is paid to the bride's family, usually a pig weighing 120 kilos. In addition to the gift of a pig, a groom must work for the bride's parents for one year. Curious about how this wedding with the whiskey and the fibers representing spirits worked with the weddings of believers of Jesus in the village, I was told that Christian weddings would not incorporate anything that would go against their new beliefs.

I was relieved to know that they did retain most of their cultural aspects of a wedding. In any mission trip that I help plan or go on myself, we are very careful to not impose western culture on the people we are serving. Our training includes emphasis on honoring our hosts and their culture, being sensitive to what is going on around us, and being slow to judge but quick to listen and learn. Much of what we experience makes sense if we just take the time to understand why it happens.

An impromptu marketplace followed where we could purchase items that the villagers had made, mostly handwoven purses, hats and belts. The evening ended with fireworks and roasting marshmallows over the fire. Roasting marshmallows was a huge hit, and something the staff and villagers had not done before. Even this was an interesting study in cultures as

Americans, who are usually experienced in this activity, would burn the marshmallows, but the Lahu would carefully and patiently roast them to a beautiful golden brown, perfectly gooey in the middle.

Our turn for fun and cultural awareness American style came the next evening. Waylon played the guitar and sang a song, but the big event was OUR skit of courtship to marriage, American style. John, from Indiana, had volunteered to take this project on, and he did a fine job of planning and choreographing an extravaganza of love and marriage. From meeting for the first time to tossing the bouquet, little was left out that was G rated. Proposing, asking the dad for his daughter's hand, purchasing the ring, and the wedding ceremony incorporated every member of the team into the hilarity. Tossing the bouquet topped off the fun, especially because we had been told that one of the ITDP staff was engaged to a young woman in the village, so the tossing was entirely rigged in her favor. The bouquet was made of shiny pipe cleaners and foam beads, truly a sight to behold!

Sunday morning dawned bright and bittersweet. It was our last day in the village. We would be leaving by 10 a.m. after breakfast, church, tear-down, and pictures at the water tank with the ITDP staff and villagers. We were tired, dirty, in love with the people we had been living with for the past week, and missing our families -- ready to go home, but not ready to leave. After our last drops of Lanna coffee were swallowed, we cleared the dishes and readied for pictures at the tank, and then church. We trekked up the hill for the last time, and many photos were taken with the tank. The stencil on the tank, designed by a member of the team, patterned off of the ITDP logo, is that of a faucet with water pouring from it into open hands, overflowing onto fields. The Bible verse, in Lahu, is John 4:13 -14. Jesus said to her, 'Everyone who drinks of this water will be thirsty again, but those who drink of the water that I will give them will never be thirsty. The water that I will give will become in them a spring of water gushing up to eternal life.'

Once picture taking was finished, we went back down the hill for church. Our long table had been transformed, everything had been stripped away except for the pile of clothing and work gloves that we were leaving for the villagers. Church was held in the common area that day instead of the closed walls of the church. We had worked with all the villagers during the week and did not want the walls of a church to be a barrier to anyone who wanted to join or watch. It was a very simple service, with prayer and song, Lahu and Americans sitting side by side. Children ran in and out, dogs sat at our feet, the sounds of chickens and pigs provided background. The bell choir of cattle and water buffalo rang as the cattle moved from the middle of the village to their grazing area. The smells of animals, cooked food with delicious spices, and fresh mountain air filled our nostrils. Kids would pop in and out, cuddling up to us for hugs and smiles; we wrapped our arms around them and held back tears. A pulpit fashioned from a small table was covered by a lace cloth and held flowers and the pastor's guitar.

Many villagers listened to the church service that day. There were testimonies from three of our team, talking about their lives and how knowing Christ changed their lives. Each translated by Mike and Witoon, even without the words, the emotion and tears of their stories touched Lahu and Americans alike. "Chief", the headman, spoke about his history with the village, and how grateful he was to have clean running water in the village and for the hard work of everyone who helped. The pastor spoke of how grateful he was that American believers came, not only to build, but to encourage the villagers. A short sermon in Lahu followed, with an offering, prayers, and singing. Both anticipating and dreading the final "amen," it did arrive, and we had to say goodbye. Villagers lined up to shake hands or hug us as we left the common area. Tears were not held back anymore as we bid each other farewell, "God bless you, thank you, I love you." We quickly changed into clothing appropriate for the journey to Chiang Mai and made our way down the hill.

    Like Pied Pipers with children running all around us, we walked down the hill to the river. Our transportation came into view -- four beautiful, handmade bamboo rafts. Some villagers had been busy preparing these for our two hour journey down the river towards Chiang Mai. Each raft held three or four people, plus experienced Lahus in the front and back for steering. We could either sit or stand as we floated down the river. Knowing that if I stood I would go head first into the river somewhere, I chose to sit. Sitting meant being wet from the waist down, but at least I could control what got wet and when. One raft had only one Lahu, and Dale (from Kearney) was elected to steer from the back. After a slight mishap, Dale became our second Lahu, following gestures from our front man on what to do. It was a fantastic ride, alternately totally quiet, surrounded by jungle, sometimes in the shade and then floating into the warm sunshine. As we approached water buffalo cooling in the water, they would stare at us and then amble to the riverbank, waiting for the foreign objects in their water to pass. Other times we would approach white water, and we would be bounced, jiggled and splashed. Dale and our guide would keep us afloat and away from the trees and rocks in our path. Two hours passed too quickly and we were soon on dry land, changing clothes and boarding the trucks to take us the rest of the way to

Running Water, Living Water

Chiang Mai.

Returning to Chiang Mai, we left the quiet rural life for the bustling city once again. We would have the remainder of Sunday to rest and Monday for some tourist activities, then Tuesday we would debrief with Mike and the ITDP staff and head to Bangkok in the evening. Returning to the hotel on Sunday, we became reacquainted with toilets that you can sit on and flush, showers that you can be naked behind with warm water, the only dirt being what was coming off our own bodies. The twin beds were glorious, soft and big, with no bug noises at our heads. A laundry was right across the street from the hotel, and we took what few clothes we had left from the village there for cleaning. Clean clothes were waiting for us at the hotel, plus other items like money, passports, and iPods that we had left there for safekeeping. Air conditioning was such a treat, and we had to choose between finding something to eat, or basking in the luxury of a bed in an air conditioned room. Food won, and several of us went to Duke's, an American food restaurant right down the street. Diet Cokes, french fries, and Mexican food were the favorites of the evening. Some of the team went night bazaar shopping, others went for massages, I went to bed. I called home to find out that my husband's retina had detached and he was going to have surgery on Tuesday. I immediately began working on plans to get home early. Our friends and daughter had things under control at home, but I wanted to be there for him. Mike could get the team on a plane on Tuesday, they didn't need me at this point. If the tickets could be exchanged for a new day, I would be out of Thailand early. My boss was working on the tickets for me, and let me know the bad news… $4000 for a one-way ticket home at best, and I wouldn't get home much earlier than planned on Wednesday. So I prayed for my husband and his doctors, and waited it out. In only two more days we would be on a plane going home.

A day of tourist activities included seeing an elephant camp, snake farm, monkey farm, and visiting a temple, after which we rested for a while then went to a Khantoke dinner dance show. Khantoke is a Lanna Thai tradition, set in an atmosphere of rich northern culture with splendid costumes and singing, including folk dancing of the hill tribe cultures. Returning from the restaurant, we needed to make our final pack for the long flight home. We were checking our luggage through to our home cities, even though we would spend a short night in Bangkok. Carry-on bags would have our quart-sized bag of 3 oz. or less containers of toiletries, one change of clothing, and anything we couldn't live without for the next thirty-six hours. We were packed by midnight, and fell asleep ready for the busy day ahead.

Our last day in Thailand! Mike was able to get one room for a late check-out, so we piled our stuff in there and headed out in the trucks to ITDP's offices. Far different than the offices I had seen previously, this building was set back from the road on a large parcel of land, where Mike's vision of coffee processing and the Lanna coffee shop will soon be realized. We gathered in the large, cozy front room to talk about our week in the village. We had been divided into groups of three in the village, instructed to write down specific observations in a journal. The observations were: ITDP staff, interaction with team and villagers, preparation, more; environment, to include food, bugs, plants, animals; family life, including gender roles, schooling, cultural influences; and finally, team interaction, including pre-trip preparation. This was a great time of remembering and talking about what we experienced. It was also an excellent way of having everyone involved in the debriefing process by including them in thinking about and recording thoughts during the entire experience.

    Following the debriefing, we were taken to different locations in Chiang Mai where the Lanna coffee is dried, processed, and roasted. Each of these processes is in a different location, hopefully soon to be relocated on the same land as the ITDP offices. Lunch was at the Lanna coffee shop, serving and selling "Mike Mann" coffee, or Lanna coffee, where we purchased pounds and pounds of different roasts -- beans and ground -- for us and our coffee-loving friends. Each of us was equipped with an empty blue duffle bag previously filled with clothing and supplies for the village experience, but now waiting for souvenirs and coffee. Keeping each bag's weight under 50 pounds did not seem to be an issue as we had left most of our clothing, our sleeping bags, and all the heavy supplies with Mike. We returned to the hotel for one last repack, adding our coffee to our checked luggage, reorganizing again, and moving all of our luggage downstairs ready to board the trucks to the airport.

    More tearful goodbyes, hugs and handshakes took place at the Chiang Mai airport. All the luggage was checked through to the United States. We would pick it up in Chicago to pass through customs before we boarded our connecting flights home. Mike met us at the airport for one last goodbye, and with that familiar twinkle in his eye he handed me a gift. Inside was something he had learned I loved…sticky rice in bamboo! It was still warm, fresh, and there was enough for everyone. It had been an enormous pleasure to work with Mike and his team, and I would miss seeing them every day. The two groups, Americans and ITDP, finally parted, and we made our way to the gate to board the plane. We settled in and began our short trip to Bangkok, where we would meet with two prearranged van drivers who would take us to the Bangkok Christian Guest House, an oasis of quiet and calm two blocks from the Patpong red light district and night bazaar, a perfect place for the team to see a little bit of Bangkok before we flew out at 6 a.m, the next morning.

Jobsite Photographs

A few simple squat toilets will improve hygiene in the village.
Photo: Angela Sudermann

Shane and Bob smooth out the bathroom floor.
Photo: Angela Sudermann

Bamboo sheet walls provide shade and privacy.
Photo: Angela Sudermann

Angela and Play Nah make roofing layers.
Photo: Michael R. Mann

Team members and villagers dig trenches together from the water source to the village. Photo: Michael R. Mann

Hugh digs trenches for the piping underneath the water tank. Photo: Angela Sudermann

It takes a village, and more, to dig miles of trench to finally get the pipe to the village. Photo: Angela Sudermann

Tying rebar means job security.
Photo: Angela Sudermann

Running Water, Living Water

Going to the hardware store is not an option. A machete and bamboo fix just about anything. Photo: Angela Sudermann

Cutting the robin's egg blue pvc pipe for the tanks.
Photo: Angela Sudermann

Dave and Ron take a break from mixing concrete.
Photo: Michael R. Mann

Sam ties rebar for an upper level of the water tank.
Photo: Angela Sudermann

Mixing concrete by hand requires a strong back, bamboo handled tools, and rubber boots. Photo: Angela Sudermann

Taking a break between bucket brigades. Photo: Angela Sudermann

Dave "Sumo" dumps a bucketful of concrete into the form.
Photo: Angela Sudermann

Filter tank (foreground) and water tank (background).
Photo: Michael R. Mann

In three days, this will be a completed water tank! Photo: Michael R. Mann

The completed water tank. Photo: Angela Sudermann

Children Photographs

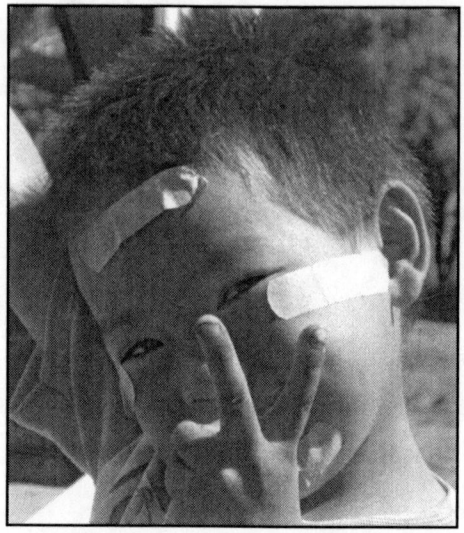

Adhesive bandages were a big hit.
Photo: Angela Sudermann

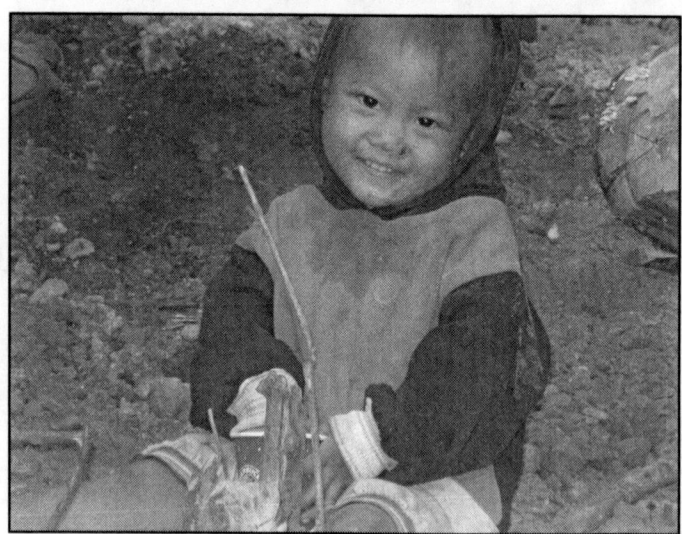

Everyone helps! Photo: Angela Sudermann

Running Water, Living Water

Bob and his puppet were entertaining for kids and adults alike.
Photo: Michael R. Mann

Angela is surrounded by children hungry for affection.
Photo: Angela Sudermann

John proudly displays his sock puppet.
Photo: Angela Sudermann

Little girls make faces for cameras around the world.
Photo: Angela Sudermann

Friends pose, and later receive the printed photo.
Photo: Angela Sudermann

Dale and Angela jump rope with the children, as one of the youngest wanders through. Photo: Angela Sudermann

Waylon sings "This Little Light of Mine" with the children. Photo: Michael R. Mann

Lahu girls love to have their photo taken! Photo: Angela Sudermann

Team Photographs

ITDP Staff and helpers pose. Photo: Michael R. Mann

Returning to Chiang Mai on bamboo rafts. Photo: Michael R. Mann

Dave and Endoo share a hug at Nightlight in Bangkok.
Photo: Angela Sudermann

Hugh and Tom on the train to Hat Yai.
Photo: Angela Sudermann

Running Water, Living Water

Discovery Team, ITDP staff, villagers, and Mike Mann in front of the completed water tower.

Village Life Photographs

Hilltop view of part of the village. Photo: Angela Sudermann

A typical home in Lahu village. Photo: Angela Sudermann

Villagers share the work of pounding rice. Photo: Michael R. Mann

Nope checks his gun while John watches.
Photo: Angela Sudermann

The Lahoo Bridge spans the river. Photo: Michael R. Mann

Grandmother in village working on her porch. Photo: Michael R. Mann

A woman returning from the field, carrying a heavy sack of rice on her back. Photo: Angela Sudermann

A typical cooking area inside a Lahu home. Photo: Michael R. Mann

Angela Sudermann

Women, too excited to wait for a faucet, open the pipe to divert the first running water to the village. Photo: Michael R. Mann

Part III: Bangkok

While we were waiting at the gate in Chiang Mai, Sam, who had been feeling very poorly for 24 hours, was feeling chilled and tired. The flight was delayed, so we had some time for him to lie down and sleep across some seats. He was running a fever and feeling weak. The unidentified spicy food he had eaten while hunting had not agreed with him at all and was taking its toll. It was disconcerting to see Sam, normally a rugged, athletic guy, lying pale and weak in the airport. We had less than twelve hours to get him feeling well enough, or at least looking well enough, to board an airplane to the states. Team members were scattered through the gate area, reading, eating, and chatting with other passengers. Some members of our group met a government lawyer who was also flying back to Bangkok. He gave the group his card, and told them if they were ever back in Bangkok to give him a call. Our flight was finally called, and the mass of people waiting to board headed for the buses that took us to our plane. Shortly after, it was wheels up to Bangkok and the first part of our journey home.

We landed in Bangkok, and as after every previous flight waited for one another at the closest large waiting area that we find. Walking at a pace Sam could keep up with, we started towards the baggage claim area where our two vans should be waiting for us. Suvarnabhumi airport is huge, and even with the moving walkways, it seems like you must walk for miles to reach your destination. Our group of twelve was spread out on the walkway, half of us near the end of the walkway closest to baggage claim, when we saw people running down the stairs and ramps toward us. Leading the way were airport personnel with radios in hand.

I initially thought they were chasing someone, but as the number of runners increased, that thought was put aside. Panicked flight attendants dressed in bright red outfits ran past us screaming as did passengers and more airport officials. Men waving radios were yelling in Thai. Every once in a while we could hear some English that sounded like "go back quickly". More and more people were running in our direction and past us, so we turned to go with them. Half of the team was still on the walkway headed towards what everyone was running from, and we yelled at them and gestured for them to turn and go back, to come our direction and hurry. That was easier said than done because they would need to walk/run faster than the walkway was moving against them. Airport personnel were also running and of absolutely no help for passengers. Storekeepers were busy pulling large shades down to close their stores. These shades are not anchored or secure, but rather just big shades like you might find in your own home. Whatever we were running from, the shades were not going to protect the merchandise. It seemed surreal to see people running and screaming from something as yet unknown, and shopkeepers standing their ground to protect their candy, overpriced duty-free items, and stuffed animals.

    Gathering the team together at the end of the walkway, we proceeded as fast as Sam could walk to a place where there were enough chairs for him to lie down. If we were going to spend time hunkered down in the airport, I was claiming some of the few comfortable seats that were there. Sam was shivering from chills, so we covered him with a blanket and fashioned a pillow out of sweatshirts. A couple of team members hit the phones right away. Others wandered a little to see what was happening and to seek information. A large group of Muslims had deplaned from a different airline about the same time as we did, and they were looking for answers and tending to some of their group who were overcome with emotion. The corridors soon emptied except for us and an occasional one or two people passing by.

After about thirty minutes of uncertainty and rumors, we confirmed with a knowledgeable-looking person that the panic was caused by large numbers of people protesting the current government. They had broken through police lines outside the airport and were now inside the airport. Our question of whether we should stay or go was answered with "you should go now, and quickly". We roused Sam as I called the van drivers to find out where they were. When they answered the phone they urged us to get out of the airport quickly and gave us their location. Thanking God that they were still waiting for us, we began moving towards the exit again. It was a long walk to baggage claim, but this time we started with far less confidence.

Instead of the sea of people that I am accustomed to in the Bangkok airport, the scene seemed grossly abnormal. Lines of police in riot gear ran past us. Reporters with video cameras were filming the scene. People lined up trying to get taxis, other people without rides, passengers with cancelled flights, and airport personnel all mingled together. What is usually controlled chaos was now out of control. We arrived at the area the van drivers stated, but couldn't find them. I called again, told them where we were, and they walked to find us. As we wove through the crowd, I fought the urge to say "hold hands and stick together" and prayed that we would all get to the vans. Passing another reporter with a camera, I heard one of the team say "You'll probably be on CNN". Realizing that the team was taking this all in stride and waving at the reporters, we reached the vans and piled in. Having no checked luggage with us made it very easy to get in the vans and get out of the airport. We drove directly to the Bangkok Christian Guest House to rest, get a handle on the situation, and prepare to fly out the next day.

  The Bangkok Christian Guest House is special to me. Located off of two busy main streets, it is nestled away from the bustle of the city while being walking distance to the skytrain, shopping, and just about anything you could want or need. I've stayed there at least once every time I have been in or through Thailand, and it is an oasis and place of rest and safety to me. It is comfort for the soul. Breakfast is provided, lunch and dinner are inexpensive and tasty, and there are meeting rooms, a chapel, and a family room to gather, relax, or meditate in. The rooms are simple, very comfortable, include western toilets and hot water, and for the first time, television in the rooms. It seemed a shame that we would be there only a few hours, but in order to "see" Bangkok, we needed to get into the city. At twenty US dollars per night, per room, we really couldn't go wrong.

  After getting everyone to their rooms with the instructions of calling them at 3 a.m. to let them know what we would be doing, I retired to my room with Angela J. and my Blackberry to monitor the situation and e-mail home. While the TV ran the news, I called my boss, e-mailed my emergency contact person, and called United Airlines. As the story unfolded, prospects dimmed for getting home Wednesday as planned. It seemed our prayer for getting through customs in Chicago was answered, perhaps not how we had envisioned! Although we had been monitoring the protest situation while we were in Chiang Mai, we did not know that the protestors had gone to the Suvarnabhumi airport the morning we left Chiang Mai, had strung barbed wire across the highway, and had been disrupting airport operations all day. We had arrived in the baggage claim area just as the protesters came into the airport building, sending everyone into a panic. There was not just a handful of protesters, though, but thousands, and the number kept growing. Men, women, children, whole families had set up camp inside the airport, vowing to stay until the sitting prime minister resigned. Protesters also 'occupied' the Don Muang airport, effectively shutting down Thailand's air traffic in and out of Bangkok. Thousands of people remained stranded inside the airport as flights continued to arrive throughout the night leaving even more passengers. We were thankful that we did get out and our van drivers had stayed to wait for us. At three in the morning I had confirmation that we would not be leaving as planned, so I called the team and told them to go back to sleep. We had an outstanding emergency contact person, Bernice, in Pennsylvania who had agreed before I left to be the one person I could e-mail with news should anything out of the ordinary occur. She would then call or e-mail the emergency contact person the team members had given me. Neither Bernice nor I expected to have to use this system, but she was very faithful and worked overtime to help get information to those who needed it.

Many things have a way of working out. Sam really wasn't fit to travel yet on Wednesday, so we took him to the hospital outpatient clinic a couple blocks from the guest house. Bangkok Christian Hospital was quite caring and efficient. We were in and out of there in two and a half hours and that included checking in, triage, diagnosis, and a two hour IV to rehydrate Sam. He was also given a bag full of medications to kill whatever bad was inside of him and to bring him back to good health. All of this at the unbelievable cost of sixty US dollars.

    The next four days alternately flew and dragged by as I tried to balance keeping the team busy with making arrangements to get out of Bangkok. We had left Chiang Mai thinking we had a few hours in Bangkok before we left for the states, so we had one change of clothes, our 3 ounce containers of toiletries, and very little money. I was carrying a large amount of Baht (Thai currency) to pay for the vans and a one-night stay in Bangkok. When plans changed, how my cash was to be spent also changed. If I could put a purchase on Visa, I did, saving the cash for emergencies. Not that twelve people stranded in Bangkok wasn't already an emergency, but we were in a comfortable guest house where we were safe and well taken care of. We laid out a plan each day to check in with me at 9 a.m., 1 p.m., and 5 p.m. If people were running low on money, they could meet me in the lobby at noon each day to eat with me and I would take care of the bill. All expenses -- hotel, food, and extras -- that were paid by me would be settled once I returned to Pennsylvania. No one was going to starve for lack of money.

    One change of clothes and 3 ounces of toiletries can last for only so long, though, and immediate needs must be taken care of by picking up bare essentials and sharing other things that we had. Ear swabs and nail clippers were passed around, as was laundry soap. I discovered that shampoo makes a suitable laundry detergent, and for once my "full body clothing" came from my shampoo, not my lack of exercise. We wondered about our checked luggage, recognizing that we might never see our stuff again. We had seen in the village how simply the Lahu lived, and now it was our turn to be unencumbered by "stuff". It was a curious feeling to be free of baggage other than what little we could carry on the plane. If only we could get rid of our emotional baggage so easily!

Registering the team with the embassy was something I had thought of before I left, but didn't do. I register whenever I travel alone, but did not take the time with this group. Thailand is safe, and nothing happens. How wrong I was! A member of my team at home got busy registering all of us with the US Embassy in Bangkok. I would now receive e-mail updates on the situation and know if the U.S. would be evacuating citizens. Another lesson learned - don't take safety in any country for granted.

Our flights were booked and rebooked a couple of times over the next few days. Rumors flew about when the siege would end, with most thinking that the protestors would be out by December 5th, the King's birthday. The King is beloved in Thailand, and to have something like this occurring on his birthday would be disgraceful. One of the guys even called the lawyer we met at the Chiang Mai airport, and he felt the same way. The United Airlines travel office was just a few blocks away and it was staying open over the weekend to accommodate all the stranded passengers. Their agents were always very polite and as helpful as possible under the circumstances, but were not getting much more information than we were, and were booking and rebooking as fast as they could. We eventually had tickets for December 3 out of Bangkok, and hoped and prayed that we would still fly out of Bangkok that morning. We stayed in contact with the United agents, and they knew us by sight, which proved to be helpful in the days to come.

The guest house is large, but small enough that you recognize people every morning at breakfast or in the lobby. Early in our extended stay in Bangkok, we met Chris and Endoo at breakfast. Chris, her husband Mark, and their five children had been in Thailand to adopt Endoo. Because paperwork had been delayed, Mark and the five children went home while Chris and Endoo stayed in Bangkok to get everything in order. That delayed Chris and Endoo in Thailand long enough for them to be caught in the airport takeover and, like us, they were stranded at the guest house.

    Chris and Endoo were a huge blessing for our team. Although Endoo is only seven years old he boosted our morale with his energy, compassion, and humor. His limbs have differing degrees of use; however he is by no means handicapped. His two prosthetic legs fit from the knee down, and include shoes which he can shake off at will. It was our delight to interact, hug, carry, chatter, and travel with him. We would often be seen in a group which included Endoo in the arms of one of the team, Chris, getting a break from carrying Endoo, and the rest of us. Usually one of us carried Endoo's legs. Chris, with her gentle and loving spirit, was an encouragement to me as she quickly became a friend and sister. We were family to Chris and Endoo, too, and they joined us in all of our activities. One of the guys nicknamed Endoo "Can Do" because of his wonderful spirit and can-do attitude. Chris and Endoo took our minds off ourselves for a couple of days until they left, getting out of Bangkok via U-Tapao, the military base two hours south of Bangkok.

    Mike Mann had been calling every day to check on us. The first time he called, he expected us to be in Tokyo or in the USA. He had hoped that we were able to get out in time, or that we had at least been able to get out of the airport. His staff had told him we had gotten out of the airport, because they had seen us on TV, waving to the news cameras as we left. Once assured that we were safe and not in need of funds, he began to work on helping us get transportation out of Bangkok. Between Mike and the team at International Ministries working on our behalf, and our friends, families and churches praying for us, we could not have been in a better 'bad situation'.

Bangkok was shut down to passenger air traffic, and the number of people stranded in Bangkok increased as the siege went on. For a number of reasons we could not return to Chang Mai for a flight out. United flights from Singapore were open but we would need to find a way there – approximately 900 miles by land through southern Thailand, Malaysia and then into Singapore. Buses and trains were booked until at least December 5th. The military opened the base in U-Tapao for a limited number of flights. That quickly became a challenging situation as 10,000 people began arriving at an airport that was not set up for passenger flights. United was not going to fly in or out of U-Tapao, so that was not an option for us. On hearing that Singapore Air had seats available for earlier than December 3rd, four of us walked to their offices to inquire about purchasing tickets. Our number was called two hours after getting in line only for the agent to tell us that they were not selling any new tickets, just rebooking current passengers. News reports suggested that even if the airport opened by the King's birthday, operations may not be back to normal for weeks because the whole airport would have to be secured, computers ramped up, and everything reapproved by the aviation agencies that secure safety. We did not want to wait until mid-December to get home. Returning to United, we changed our Bangkok tickets to Singapore, confirmed for December 2, holding seats for December 3 and 4. But how would we get to Singapore? We had to solve that within 36 hours, or change tickets again. This time, United may not be as accommodating.

I worked within our system and with our partners, using trusted agencies and learning more about the regions we would need to travel through. Southern Thailand and Malaysia are predominately Muslim, with southern Thailand having some militant groups which had caused trouble for Christians in the past. Twelve Americans are fairly obvious overseas, and I sought a solution that would minimize risk and get us home as soon as possible. Three members of the team were independently seeking a way out of Bangkok and chose to leave on their own. We prayed for their safety and tearfully sent them on their way. They arrived safely in the U.S. almost exactly 24 hours before we did.

During our time in Bangkok, I figured we should be productive, so I called Jeff and Annie Dieselberg, ABC missionaries who invited us to see them Friday to learn about Nightlight. Annie and Jeff serve in Bangkok, a bustling metropolis of more than ten million people. Annie founded and is CEO of NightLight Design Co., Ltd., a business-as-mission which employs and empowers women who would otherwise be involved in the sex trade industry in Bangkok. For many years Annie has had a passion for ministering to the women working as bar girls and/or prostitutes in Bangkok. The Nightlight ministry has grown from that, and has also become a business in which women from the bars can have an alternative way to earn an income by making fine jewelry. Eighty women who had previously been selling themselves in the bars are currently employed at Nightlight where they gain self-esteem, learn that they are beautiful children of God, and are paid a fair wage with benefits, have child care, and enjoy a safe and caring workplace.

The group that visited Nightlight had an eye-opening

introduction to Bangkok's sex trade, and what two missionaries are doing to help change the lives of women in the bars of Bangkok. Jeff had received an e-mail that morning asking him to visit an American in the hospital. When he presented the opportunity to the group, three fellows jumped at the chance to minister to someone who was alone in the city. They had an incredible experience, and felt like we did so many other times during the trip, that we were there for "such a time as this".

International Ministries (IM) has partner organizations with whom mutually beneficial relationships have developed around the world. In Thailand, the Church of Christ in Thailand (CCT) is the umbrella organization over the Thailand Baptist Missionary Fellowship (TBMF). CCT is not the same as the Church of Christ in the USA, but works with many denominations and many countries. The connections Mike made between the manager of the guest house and the folks at CCT who had connections with trusted travel agencies were another answer to prayers. Within hours the nine of us had train tickets on a sleeper car, and a private van driver to take us all the way from Hat Yai in southern Thailand to a hotel in Singapore, where the travel agent had booked us rooms already. We could enjoy one day of rest in Singapore before departng at 6:40 a.m. on December 3rd, connecting with the same flights that we had scheduled for November 27th, only exactly one week later.

Train reservations had been made so quickly that several of us had laundry, still wet from doing our daily wash in the sink that morning. Just 90 minutes after we learned about the train to Malaysia we were picked up at the guest house. We hastily gathered our things, grabbed some lunch, and settled our bill at the guest house. Our guardian angel from CCT arrived with tickets for five lower berths and four upper. We were soon to be in territory even I had never experienced, leading eight others who thankfully trusted God and me to get us safely home. I was relying heavily on God and the great kindness of people we were meeting in Thailand, plus those who were supporting us at home. My Blackberry was my constant companion. I was receiving encouraging e-mails from co-workers and friends back home and phone calls from Mike who continued to check on us. I felt strangely at ease and at peace with the plan we had been given. Our CCT contact got us settled on the train, spoke to the steward so that he would take care of us and not let us get off the train too early, and bid us goodbye. The travel agent met us on the train where he and I completed our transaction for the van ride to follow, telling me who to look for, the number of the van, and leaving me with his business card should I need him again. Our CCT angel returned to the train with a box of Dunkin' Donuts, warm pastries filled with meat, and a roll of toilet paper. We would be able to purchase meals on the train, but the Dunkin' Donuts were a happy treat and were eaten quickly.

Even before the train left the station I needed to locate the bathroom. Anyone that has been out in public with me knows that I have an internal magnet that must find the first available rest room. Perhaps it's my punishment for laughing at my mother whenever she had to stop at a gas station's rest room when we went shopping. Having been on trains overseas, I knew what to expect of a railroad bathroom and was not to be disappointed. It had not been stocked with supplies yet, so I was glad that I had my trusty Kleenex in my pocket. The toilet was stainless steel and the flusher was a pedal on the floor. The use of the flusher was more of a quick cleaner, however, because anything that went into the toilet went directly onto the ground below. With the train at a standstill, imagination is not required about what is happening in the car above, but at 60 miles per hour, well, you can guess the physics.

The train ride was to last 16 hours, all but three in darkness. We were finally situated two to a mini-compartment, one person facing another, until the top and bottom beds were unfolded and made up. Three hooks near the window were perfect for wet laundry. Wet shirts were a perfect cover for wet underwear, enabling us to get our laundry out to dry without offending our neighbors. We stopped at several stations on our way out of town, and at each stop I prayed there would be no protestors. Those who ordered food were served dinner, then the stewards came by to make up the beds. We were tucked in by 8 p.m. and happy to be able to stretch out. Our beds were made private with a curtain, enabling us to spread our wet laundry out. The night was fairly comfortable, the rhythmic clacking of the train and the swaying of the car lulling me to sleep. The temperature alternated between hot and cold so the cuddly blanket they provided was either off or on, and the air freshener they sprayed at regular intervals could make your eyes water. Considering the alternative, the air freshener was a welcome addition. Finally, about 5 a.m., I could not sleep anymore. I grabbed my toothpaste, water bottle, and Kleenex and headed to the bathroom.

    The bathroom was a wet mess, like someone had taken a shower there. The walls were all wet, water was on the floor, and even the toilet seat was drenched. The cause of the problem was obvious. It was pouring rain through an open window. I finished up there and proceeded to the sink outside the toilet area. The sink area is for common use, with two sinks and a large mirror for passengers and crew alike to freshen up. It is located at the end of the car. The doors were open, allowing a nice breeze to blow in. The roadbed seemed particularly rocky, which made brushing teeth a memorable experience you just can't achieve in a stationary site. By a combination of leaning, balancing, and timing coordinated with the sway of the train, I was able to get my teeth brushed without injuring myself or the guy next to me. Back at my seat, I watched out the window as the rain continued. It must have been raining for quite a while, because the roads and fields were flooding, In just two hours we would pull into Hat Yai and meet our van driver.

    The train rolled into Hat Yai in the pouring rain. We gathered our bags and made our way to the area where others awaited transportation. We were approached many times by people who wanted to take us somewhere, but we were looking for someone with my name on a card. Unfortunately, no one matched that description. After calling Mike, who called someone, who called someone else, we found our driver who had just arrived. We piled into the van, sadly denying a couple who wanted to board the van as well. The driver introduced himself as Toh Nee (Tony), and then "Handsome Tony". He was friendly, fun, extremely competent, and as we would find out, loyal to us and his mission to get us to Singapore.

    First he had to get us out of Hat Yai, and the streets were flooding. Tony made detour after detour until he was able to get us out of town and onto higher ground. Forty minutes later we were at the Thai border with Tony instructing us on the proper procedure for getting through immigration, including no cameras, emphasizing 'NO'. That accomplished, we boarded the van again and drove a short distance to go through the immigration process in Malaysia. Again, no cameras, as we grabbed our bags and passports to enter Malaysia. Back in the van, we drove another short distance to a rest stop where we could exchange our Baht into ringgits, formerly the Malaysian dollar, and grab some breakfast. Handsome Tony gave us fifteen minutes and we chose an assortment of food: some eggs, some rice, some snack foods. One cookie that Dave purchased tasted like those orange circus peanuts we get in the U.S. Our fifteen minutes passed quickly and we boarded the van for our long day through Malaysia.

The rain stopped and we were able to view Malaysia in sunlight. The highways were clean, wide, and smooth. Traffic flowed well, and Tony was able to make good time. We enjoyed the scenery, the green foliage, the farms, different crops and buildings. We passed and were passed by motorcycles, family cars, pickups, commercial haulers and logging trucks.

Total time in the van was expected to be 14 hours. It was a tight fit, but the guys were in good spirits, and I could hear some version of "Name that Tune" and other musical quizzes going on in the back seats. There was much singing, lyric checks, and laughter as we journeyed south. Handsome Tony had a TV screen for the back seats, and he put a DVD of the Eagles Tour on for entertainment. The guys sang along and reminisced, passing the time quickly. After a couple of hours it was time to stop to stretch our legs, get coffee, and use the restrooms. Restrooms were astoundingly clean and neat along the highway in Malaysia. Easily three dozen stalls – both squatties and western style with toilet paper -- and large sinks available for washing ourselves. Coffee shops, tourist shops, various fast food eateries, and even a Dunkin'

Donuts were available. All locations were well marked, including the prayer room. Each rest area we stopped at included a Muslim prayer room. Walking back to the van, Dave caught my eye. He was sitting on a bench and looked pale and weak. I stopped to chat and see how he was doing before we got back in the van. He excused himself and walked quickly back to the restrooms. When he returned, we realized that he was quite sick to his stomach. I left to look for some ginger ale or cola, and eventually found Pepsi and ginger beer. I brought it back, giving even Dave a kick out of the ginger beer. We opened it and sniffed it. It was not beer, but indeed a ginger drink of some sort, so we determined it might be good for Dave's tummy and he started sipping away. We piled back in the van, with Dave in the front seat next to Handsome Tony, and away we drove.

  Another DVD amused us for two more hours, then not too far down the road, Dave indicated that he needed us to pull over - NOW. Tony couldn't do that, so we provided the next best thing available - a plastic bag. What surprised all of us was that his action into the plastic bag didn't cause a chain reaction, a smell, nor did it cause Tony to pull over at the next available stop to toss the bag in the trash. We all knew it was there, though, kind of like the elephant in the room no one will talk about. We felt terrible for Dave and did our best to keep him comfortable. Ron's anti-diarrhea meds, the ginger beer, the cola, nothing seemed to help Dave as the day became night, and we rolled further and further towards Singapore.

  Nighttime was very very dark as we continued our travel through the countryside, seeing only the lights of passing cars and an occasional building. One of the guys looked out the window on the right side of the van and spotted the sky smiling at us. While

Running Water, Living Water

they grabbed their cameras and exclaimed how amazing it was, I tried to scramble my way to that side of the van to see for myself. Twisting around the seats and looking out the window, I confirmed that the sky was indeed smiling at us. A beautiful crescent moon, with Jupiter and Venus just a few degrees apart and above the moon, gave the appearance of a smiley face in the sky. There were no other stars visible, so to our eyes and minds, it was very clear that God was smiling at us. Handsome Tony told us that he heard on the news that this was supposed to happen, and it wasn't till we returned to the states that I read about how rare this astronomical phenomenon was. We will always believe that God was smiling on us that night. We had made it out of Bangkok, we were within a few hours of Singapore, and would be home in two days. Protesters had kept us from leaving Bangkok on our timetable, but through prayer, wonderful people helping us, and our faith that God would show us a way out, we were leaving in safety and having a great experience along the way.

Leaving Malaysia was easy, and a quick trip down the road brought us to the Singapore immigration post. For the first time all day we were in a crowd of people. The building was spotless, organized, and the process was efficient. We got through reasonably quickly and headed back to the van. Tony was usually at the van waiting for us at rest stops and immigration, but this time there was no sign of him there. A couple calls to Mike, and half an hour later, we saw Tony walking our direction. He said something about a lot of paperwork and having to be back at immigration in two and a half hours. I can only imagine what he had to go through to get permission to take us into Singapore. He continued to be an amazing guy, good humored and protective of us.

Singapore is a city-state, and it wasn't long at all before we were in the heart of the city with its pristine streets and hundreds of lit construction cranes reaching into the sky. Still in the night sky, they sparkled, pointed in different directions, in different heights, it looked like a bizarre space-age garden. It was quite beautiful, and accented the twinkling skyscrapers and massive ferris wheel planted in the city. Harbor lights lit up the sky as well, giving the city a magical quality that would have been fun to explore had we not been exhausted from our 30-hour journey from Bangkok. It was after 10 p.m. when we arrived at the Bencoolen Hotel, and the usual directed chaos began as we unloaded the van, thanked Handsome Tony and sent him on his way, and tried to get checked into our rooms. The first room was for Dave and Hugh, and they were sent straight upstairs so that Dave could go to bed. The rest of us were sorted out in short order with instructions to meet at 9 a.m. the next morning.

  Being the only female in the group now, I had my own room, and headed there long after everyone else had departed to theirs. When I stepped inside the elevator the door closed. I punched the button for the ninth floor. Nothing happened. I repeated the action. Nothing happened again. Because doing it a third time would certainly make a difference, I punched the button once again. Nothing happened for the third time. So there I stood inside a closed elevator, and nothing was working. I was NOT going to walk all those steps to my room. I couldn't. Thank goodness two angels came to my rescue. The door opened, and a young couple stepped in. They took their room card, passed it over a contraption on the wall, and miraculously the buttons all worked! I laughed and explained what I had been doing in the elevator, and they patiently explained how to operate it, but also suggested that I should use the passenger elevator, not the freight lift. The next morning, I noticed that all instructions were in English. Had I bothered to read them I would have known what to do. I got to my room and fell into bed around 1 a.m. looking forward to a good night's sleep.

Around 3 a.m. a phone was ringing, music was playing, or an alarm was going off somewhere. I fumbled around and finally woke up enough to realize it was my cell phone. I stumbled out of bed and grabbed it just as the ringing stopped. I didn't recognize the number, but placed the phone next to my pillow and tried to go back to sleep. I had just drifted off when the phone rang again. I answered and a female voice asked for Waylon Woods. I told her I didn't know where he was, but I thought he was probably sleeping in his room. She identified herself as a reporter from Hastings, Nebraska, and wanted to interview Waylon. She asked what time it was. When I told her 3 a.m., she exclaimed, "I am so sorry, I was told you had only a one-hour-time difference! I'll call back later". I thought that was a good idea, so I bid her goodbye and went back to sleep.

Breakfast was served in an open-air sidewalk area, where there is a kitchen, buffet food tables, and four dining tables, each of which had four chairs. Next to the hotel was a bar, and then a Muslim prayer room. In the daylight the streets of Singapore were everything we had heard they were -- clean, well maintained, and skyscrapers as far as the eye could see. After our meeting we spread out to explore the city. Money needed to be exchanged, souvenirs purchased, legs stretched, and with nothing to do and no worries, the only guidelines were don't get arrested, and be back by five o'clock to check in.

Everyone had a great time in Singapore that day doing whatever they wanted. We gathered in the hotel lobby to compare notes. A couple of us napped, some were sporting new t-shirts, and some had walked the city. It was time to decide where to eat for dinner. There is an old joke, "what do you get when you put five Baptists in a room? Ten opinions." That was what it was like to decide where to eat. Ron and I went to check on Dave, and some of the others left for different restaurants. By my sheer will Dave was to recover by 4 a.m. the next morning - he would to be on that plane to Tokyo! I was relieved that he looked much better than when I last saw him, and he even asked for a little something to eat. Four of us went to eat together and on the way back picked up some peanut butter crackers for Dave. With instructions to everyone to meet in the lobby at 4:15 a.m., I headed back to my room and to bed.

Our flight to Tokyo was uneventful, and we were able to have a nice time debriefing at an empty gate before we had to say goodbye to Hugh, who would fly to San Francisco shortly before we left for Chicago. We had heard that Chicago weather could be snowy, so we prayed that we would get out of Chicago and home as scheduled. Once we landed in Chicago, I had 45 minutes to clear immigration and customs, and get to my flight to Philadelphia. When the plane landed, I bid a quick and sad farewell to the guys and ran to immigration, grateful that I did not have my checked luggage! Having very little with me shortened the time spent in customs and I made it to my gate just in time to board the plane. Praying that the snow falling then would not get any worse, I settled into my seat and closed my eyes. When the engines roared to life, I breathed a sigh of relief. I was going home.

REFLECTIONS

As I write this, I've been back in the United States for a month. I'm back in the routine of daily life in Pennsylvania, but once again my life has been changed by a few weeks in Thailand. I have been surprised, and I have new people lodged in my heart for eternity. When I think of the ITDP staff, the Lahu in the village, Chris and Endoo at the guest house, the people who made our travel out of Thailand possible, Mike Mann and the team from the USA, I smile. When I look at the pictures I want to tell the story of each one to anyone who will listen.

I want to share the story of this small Lahu village and their vision of healthier lives for the community. I want to share how a dedicated group of hill tribe men and women serve in a ministry called ITDP to help villages realize that vision. I want to tell people to go to Thailand and experience the wonderful hospitality, the amazing food, and the beautiful country. They should share in the work of Mike Mann as ITDP continues to work with villages through water and sanitation, agricultural, educational, medical projects and much more.

This was the first mission trip that I led. I had never wanted to lead a trip and was sure I would be horrible at it, but with a lot of help, I did it. Family, friends, colleagues, and my church family were praying for me. My prayer requests had been for patience, that my words would be full of grace, that I could make wise decisions, and that I would be culturally sensitive. The American team, the ITDP staff, and the Lahu villagers accepted each other, learned from one another, and became brothers and sisters of the heart. I learned about myself as I interacted with each group. As a team leader I was delighted by how easily the days progressed and how well everyone got along. As a member of the team, I felt part of something meaningful that would change lives in Thailand and the United States.

Looking back, I think about what I should have done differently. The truth is, there wasn't really much that I did that made this trip what it was. Sure, I designed the brochure, posted the information on the Internet, and talked about it at conferences, but my words were to open listeners of a team that was handpicked by God. God worked not only in the hearts of eleven people in Oregon, Nebraska, and Indiana, but also in the hearts of people in a small village in northern Thailand, a Lahu village without running water but with a vision of a healthier life. This was a village with a handful of believers in Jesus Christ and a young Lahu pastor who led them with a vision of running water, and the living water of Jesus Christ flowing through their lives. Both groups prepared for a week which would change their lives forever.

Mike Mann became a special friend, brother, and hero to me and the group. I would lead a team with him and ITDP again.

Immanuel, meaning "God is with us," describes our week in Bangkok. Although I knew it at the time, I really felt the impact of it when I returned home where Advent had begun and Immanuel was the theme. Our week in Bangkok was completely unexpected, but never once did we feel unsafe, uncomfortable, or abandoned. At times, I felt like Paul when he was trying to get into Asia to tell the story of Jesus and kept bumping into obstacles, the difference being that Paul was trying to get in and we were trying to get out. Brought into a situation where the options were total trust in others or depending on our own devices, it became clear that our own human efforts continued to be in vain. As it turned out, our way was narrow, defined, and very clear providing that we took one day and one step at a time, trusting our future to God and others. When I visualize our time in Bangkok, I see our path lit by prayers, guided by people whose kindness overwhelmed us, encouraged by e-mails, blessed by angels in the form of Chris and Endoo, the guest house and CCT staff, travel agents, van drivers, and train stewards. Immanuel, God with us.

A mission trip isn't finished when we get home; it begins in a new way. I've heard from members of the team who are speaking in churches and organizations in their communities. Their passion for Thailand, the hill tribe people, and the work of ITDP came from heeding that small voice of God that said, "GO." I think it was said best by Shane in an e-mail to me after the trip. He said, "…Anyway, I have a whole lot to think about and process in my mind and heart. I will never be satisfied with the level of mission involvement I had before. No longer can I be happy just throwing money at missions. Going means SOOOO much more! It was truly the experience of a lifetime, but it was only the first!! I'm looking forward to many more mission trips and a long, fruitful relationship with ITDP."

It was such a privilege to be a part of this experience. I am additionally blessed to be able to work at International Ministries, where I can serve volunteers every day, helping them follow the call to "Go."

If you were moved by the situation of the hill tribe people, there are some things you can do to help.

- Support Mike Mann through International Ministries. Purchasing this book is a start. Royalties from the sale of this book go to Mike Mann's financial support. Visit www.internationalministries.org/missionaries/mike_mann to read more about Mike and to donate online.

- Support the ministry of Integrated Tribal Development Project through International Ministries.

- Support the ministry of Annie and Jeff Dieselberg and Nightlight Design, Co. Ltd. Visit www.internationalministries.org/missionaries/dieselberg to read more about Annie and Jeff, and www.nightlightinternational.com to learn more about Nightlight and human trafficking.

- Pass this book along, or better yet, purchase another one for a friend. Raise the awareness of the millions of people around the world that do not have access to clean water. Without clean water, children die from diarrhea, and other very preventable diseases.

- Get children involved! Use the idea of a "water project" for a Vacation Bible School, Sunday School, or School project. Raise awareness, funds, get connected with a village in Thailand. Contact International Ministries for more information.

- GO! There are several trips a year that go to Thailand to serve with Mike and ITDP. Help bring running water to homes and the Living Water of Jesus to lives.
  Email bimvolunteers@abc-usa.org or call 1-800-222-3872 ext 2366 for more information.

LaVergne, TN USA
13 January 2010
169811LV00002B/82/P